ANGELS

MASTER OF FLEMALLE. *Nativity*. Ca. 1420. Musée des Beaux-Arts, Dijon.

ANGELS

BY

JAMES UNDERHILL

INTRODUCTION BY

GERHARD BOTT

ELEMENT
Shaftesbury, Dorset ● Rockport, Massachusetts
Brisbane, Queensland

This edition published in Great Britain in 1995 by Element Books Limited

Published in Great Britain in 1995 by
Element Books Limited
Shaftesbury, Dorset SP7 8BP

Published in the USA in 1995 by
Element Books, Inc.
42 Broadway, Rockport, MA 01966

Published in Australia in 1995 by
Element Books Limited
for Jacaranda Wiley Limited
33 Park Road, Milton, Brisbane 4064

Design by Studio 31
Printed in Italy

British Library Cataloguing in Publication
data available

Library of Congress Cataloging in Publication
data available

ISBN 1-85230-750-1 Paperback edition
ISBN 1-85230-757-9 Hardcover edition

CONTENTS

RAPHAEL. *Angel Holding an Inscription* fragment from the *Altarpiece of St. Nicholas of Tolentino.*
1501. Louvre, Paris.

FRENCH SCHOOL. *Wilton Diptych.* Ca. 1395. National Gallery, London.

GERARD DAVID. *The Annunciation.* 1506. Metropolitan Museum of Art. Bequest of Mary Stillman Harkness, 1950. (50.145.9a)

ANGELS

AN

INTRODUCTION

e appears before us, as if he had just at that moment arrived from his heavenly dwelling place. His right hand is raised in greeting; his left hand holds a scepter, the symbol of his authority. He is dressed in a long flowing robe and a richly embroidered cape. His powerful wings are wonderfully detailed. Serene and compassionate, he is Gabriel, angel of the Annunciation. This work was painted at the beginning of the sixteenth century by the Flemish master Gerard David.

Two naked infants, with colored wings and tangled hair, lean on the lower frame of a painting. These childlike angels are called *putti*. They glance mischievously at the figure of St. Barbara. She kneels on a cloud, which represents the heavenly sphere, and worships a lovely Madonna holding the Christ child. Saint Sixtus completes this devotional tableau. His finger points outward, beckoning the viewer into the painting. Completed in 1512, the *Sistine Madonna* is one of Raphael's best-known works.

Mary, depicted as a young girl, kneels on the ground in a rocky grotto. It is twilight. With one hand she enfolds the young child, John the Baptist, while her other hand reaches toward her Son, who sits before her, his right hand raised. A winged youth clad in a flowing robe sits behind the Christ child; he points with his right forefinger to John. Leonardo da Vinci executed two versions of this subject. It is not derived directly from the Bible, since nowhere in the scripture is there described a meeting of Jesus and John as children; the scene is the artist's invention. It is entitled *The Madonna of the Rocks*.

In the fifteenth century Albrecht Dürer created a powerful series of woodcuts based on the Apocalypse as described in the Book of Revelation. The series is populated with strong and solemn angelic figures. Dürer, like Leonardo, does not slavishly follow scripture. Rather he presents his own vivid interpretation of the biblical text that accompanies each woodcut. Dürer's depiction of St. Michael slaying the dragon shows the archangel, whose figure takes up almost the entire composition, as a mighty warrior. His countenance is stern and awe-inspiring. In another print from the series, four angels with sharp swords cut down a group of sinners, which includes popes and emperors, massed below them. Dürer's militant angels are fearsome human figures who perform God's will with zeal.

These works exemplify how the language of art brings to life the idea that angels appear in many different forms. Traditionally, angels were considered to be ethereal beings who acted as intermediaries between heaven and earth. They provided artists with an opportunity to portray heavenly things and the execution of God's will on earth. And in so doing artists made angels tangible, giving concrete form to these disembodied beings. As the forms of artistic expression evolved, the depictions and imaginings of angels underwent a parallel transformation. Over the centuries, changing representations of angels have expressed and provoked changing ideas about their very nature. Moreover, the history of the idea of angels is an important chapter in the history of Western art.

Angels first appear in the Old Testament, where we learn of their acts and powers. They are also found throughout the New Testament and in the Apocrypha (texts from the Old Testament that are not included in all versions of the Bible). These holy books do not, however, tell us much about what angels look like. When Abraham is visited by three men who we realize are angels, they are not described further. Nor are any particulars given

RAPHAEL. *The Sistine Madonna.* (detail) Ca. 1512. Gemäldegalerie Alte Meister, Dresden.

LEONARDO DA VINCI. *Madonna of the Rocks.* Ca. 1483–1495. Louvre, Paris.

ALBRECHT DÜRER. *Four Avenging Angels.* 1498. British Museum, London.

about the angels that appear to Jacob in his dream. Tobias meets an angel at his front door, but neither he nor his father has any idea of the angel's identity until the angel reveals himself to them.

In the New Testament, Gabriel, the angel of the Annunciation, is not described. We know only he appears to Mary. Mary is not frightened by him but is surprised at his greeting and news. And when the angel draws near the shepherds to announce the birth of the Christ child, we learn that "the glory of the Lord shone round about them" (Luke 2:9). The Gospel of Matthew, recounting events that took place after the Crucifixion, tells us: "And, behold, there was a great earthquake: for the angel of the Lord descended from heaven, and came and rolled back the stone from the door [of Christ's sepulchre] and sat upon it" (Matt. 28:2). Matthew also records how an angel protected the infant Jesus by warning Joseph in a dream that Herod was planning an attempt on the child's life. The angel commands Joseph to take flight to Egypt. We never learn, however, in what guise this angel appears to Joseph.

Other books of the New Testament offer a few more details about angels. When the disciples witness Christ rising into heaven, two men "in white apparel" come to them and strengthen them in their faith (Acts 1:9–11). St. John the Divine says that the Book of Revelation was sent to him from God by his angel. He speaks of many angels in the Book of Revelation and describes their appearance and attributes.

The Judeo-Christian scriptural tradition also hints at a hierarchical ordering of angels. It suggests that archangels stand near to God and that each nation has its own angel in heaven. Israel, for example, is under the care of the archangel Michael. Individuals, too, are watched over by their guardian angels.

These ideas were expanded upon by a Christian mystic, Dionysius the Areopagite, who created the foundation of angelology, the study of angels. In his book *The Celestial Hierarchy,* written around 500 A.D., Dionysius delineates nine orders of angels arranged in three ranks. The first rank consists of seraphim, cherubim, and thrones; the second of dominions, powers, and authorities; and the third of principalities, archangels, and angels. Each order is described in detail. The seraphim are beings of "penetrating warmth" while the cherubim have the gift to see and know God. The cherubim share their vision with "an outpouring of wisdom." Dionysius's classification became highly elaborated in the Middle Ages and was the source of later speculation on the nature of angels and many of the attributes assigned to them in art.

In the thirteenth century, St. Thomas Aquinas made use of Dionysius's scheme in his speculations on angels found in the *Summa Theologica.* But where *The Celestial Hierarchy* was a visionary's description of the heavens, Aquinas sought to derive the philosophical and theological implications underlying it.

Aquinas looked upon each rank of angels as defining a particular relationship to

God. Thus the angels of the first rank (seraphim, cherubim, and thrones) are entirely turned toward God. They know Him through direct contemplation. Angels of the second rank (dominions, powers, and authorities) know God through their contemplation of the causes underlying all phenomena. They contemplate principles and ideas. Angels of the third rank are concerned with human affairs. Principalities oversee nations, archangels appear to individuals on momentous occasions, and angels watch over individuals. Thus angels of the third rank know God through his creation and are furthest from direct knowledge of Him.

The earliest Christian art, in part following scriptural tradition, portrays angels as grown men or youths, without any specific attributes. Early Christian sarcophagi and ivories picture angels as solemn young men. Over time, artists attached certain characteristics to these heavenly spirits: angels acquired halos and wings; the halos represented virtue and innocence. The wings signified that angels were messengers who traveled between heaven and earth. In fact the word "angel" derives from the Greek word for messenger. Since they had to "fly" from heaven to earth, they needed wings for their passage. The earliest winged angel we know of is found in a fifth-century mosaic in the Church of St. Prudencia in Rome. In an Annunciation scene from the following century we first see Gabriel pictured as flying with wings. A winged angel dating from about the same period accompanies Elijah into heaven, in a wood carving that decorates the door of the Church of St. Sabina in Rome. From the fifth century on, artists inevitably included wings when they sought to portray angels. There are, naturally, a few exceptions, particularly in the Renaissance works of Michelangelo and Piero della Francesca.

So it's not surprising that the contemporary observer looking at Gerard David's beautiful painting immediately recognizes an angel. That the little naked figures in Raphael's *Sistine Madonna* and the kneeling figure in Da Vinci's *Madonna of the Rocks* are angels is also unmistakably clear. And one does not have to read the text accompanying Dürer's woodcut series on the Apocalypse to identify the striking winged spirits that populate its pages.

In Greek and Roman art we also find winged figures with human features. Thanatos, the son of Night and brother of Sleep, has, as befits the God of Death, wings that he spreads over the newly departed. Sirens and harpies are winged birdlike female figures. Hermes, the messenger of the gods, is depicted with wings on his helmet or on his feet. In the famous sculpture of Nike in the Louvre, the Goddess of Victory spreads her wings. Good genii are always depicted with wings in classical art, as are Eros and Cupid figures.

But these mythic beings have at best a collateral relation to Christian and Jewish angels. In the classical Greek and Roman worlds there was no separation between the gods and the natural world of men. Gods and demigods moved and acted within the sphere of human activity while at the same time ruling over it from heaven. There was no

GUARIENTO. *Archangel.* Ca. 1350. Museo Civico, Padua. (Granger Collection, NY)

need for angels, since the gods themselves regularly came down to earth to further their own designs. Many of the gods had dwelling places on earth, and Greek mythology constantly dealt with personal interactions between gods and men. Nonetheless, classical motifs made themselves felt in depictions of angels, particularly in Renaissance art, where they joined with religious ideas to create a new vision of the angel, which was one imbued with earthly qualities.

The forerunners of biblical angels can be found in Babylonian and other Near Eastern religions. Throughout this area there was a belief in the existence of beings, inferior in rank to the gods, who were used as messengers to carry divine commands down to earth. Angels also play an important role in Islam. It is an angel named Jibreel (Gabriel) who brings the Qur'an to Mohammed: "For surely he revealed it to your heart by Allah's command, verifying that which is before it and guidance and good news for the believers" (II.97). He is described as having 140 pairs of wings.

Because of powerful prohibitions in orthodox Islam against attempts to picture God and man, there is no tradition of depicting angels in most Islamic art. The Shiite branch of Islam, which flourished in Persia, relaxed these restrictions and starting in the eleventh century produced many graceful representations of angelic beings.

In keeping with the highly stylized nature of Byzantine art, Byzantine angels were seen as large, static figures dressed in long robes. Byzantine mosaics and illuminated manuscripts emphasized their otherworldly nature. This monumentality influenced early medieval art in the West, where angels evolved from young men to bearded superhuman figures with gigantic wings.

Over the course of several centuries the artistic conception that proclaimed the transcendent nature of angels gradually changed to one that viewed angels as more human. One piece of evidence pointing to this change is that angels began to wear priestly robes, thus bringing them somewhat closer to the human realm. Artists in the time of the Crusades even went so far as to portray angels as knights clothed in armor. Especially beloved was St.

ARTIST UNKNOWN. *Archangel Jibreel.* 14th century. (Granger Collection, New York)

ARTIST UNKNOWN. Illumination from an English Gospel of St. Matthew. 11th century.
(Granger Collection, NY)

GIANLORENZO BERNINI. *The Ecstasy of St. Theresa.* 1645–1652. Santa Maria della Vittoria, Rome. (Art Resource, NY)

IL GUERCINO. *Virgin and Child with the Patron Saints of Modena.* Ca. 1651. Louvre, Paris.

Michael, a courageous warrior in the fight against evil and the patron of the Holy Roman Empire.

Art had a very important teaching function in the Middle Ages, as the greater part of congregations were illiterate. The great Gothic cathedrals were religious texts carved in stone. Concurrently, the artistic rendering of the life of Christ from the Nativity to the Resurrection became more grounded in the details of everyday existence. The conception and depiction of angels changed accordingly. Whether presented as messengers, warriors, or servants, angels no longer stood isolated in a heavenly sphere. They played out their parts in realistically conceived landscapes or domestic interiors drawn from medieval contemporary life. Art had brought angels down into the human world.

In Giotto's famous fresco cycle (ca. 1300) that decorates the Arena Chapel in Padua, we encounter the first unclothed angel. Here too we see for the first time angelic musicians. They play contemporary instruments and, much like a church choir, sing the praises of God. Angels also hold the instruments of Christ's suffering; they are full participants in the Nativity and in all the details of the Incarnation.

The revolutionary effects brought about by the Renaissance in Italian and Flemish painting included the discovery of scientific perspective and the technique of oil painting. The outpouring of creative energy is astonishing; the work of this period continues to have a decisive influence on artists' aims and expectations. It was a time of prodigious artistic achievement: Van Eyck painted his *Adoration of the Lamb;* Raphael, the *School of Athens* and his many beautiful Madonnas; Leonardo, the *Last Supper;* and Michelangelo, the ceiling of the Sistine Chapel and the *Last Judgment.*

Angels are seemingly everywhere. Renaissance artists used the figure of the angel to express their most exalted conceptions of beauty. The inspired character of the works was joined with a new appreciation for the human form, which was a part of the rediscovered legacy of classical antiquity. From Gerard David's beautiful, grave beings of holiness to Raphael's heroic St. Michael, Renaissance angels are embodied light, victorious and glorified beings.

At the same time, seeds were planted that would lead to a gradual degeneration in the seriousness of the angelic figure. Putti — little childlike angels — make their first appearance and soon are widespread. Angels become decidedly more feminine, softer, and less majestic.

The Protestant Reformation, begun by Martin Luther at the beginning of the sixteenth century, wrought radical changes in the conceptual and artistic consciousness of the period. Angels become even more familiar. They were depicted as brothers or neighbors who come to offer help in times of need. Like the long-dead saints, whose scenes of martyrdom were pictured against contemporary backdrops, angels are seen as living contemporaries. Both angels and saints become exemplars for the Christian struggling in his daily life.

DANTE GABRIEL ROSSETTI. *Ecce Ancilla Domini.* 1850. Tate Gallery, London.
(Art Resource, NY)

The ecstatic quality of sixteenth-century mannerism with its attenuated figures and extreme coloration, offered angels rapt in contemplation. Meanwhile, the strong Counter-Reformation stressed the militancy of angels, who were seen as witnesses or participants in the bloody religious conflicts of the era.

Baroque art was above all sensuous. Its angels were luxuriant beings, decidedly of this world. This treatment is perhaps most clearly seen in the wildly exaggerated angelic figures in Bernini's *Altar of St.Theresa* in the Church of Santa Maria della Victoria in Rome. Bernini's figures on the Bridge of Angels in Rome are infused with seductive sensuality. These are earthly, not heavenly, creatures. The solemn, transcendent angel of the Middle Ages had given way to an often ostentatious representation of strength and beauty. Angels now combined in themselves the innocence of young boys and the budding sexuality of young girls. Such depictions departed further and further from the concepts derived from biblical teachings, but they were considered more artistic.

In the last stage of this continuum, angels were cut loose from all scriptural moorings. By the mid-eighteenth century they became decorative and ornamental figures, made to adorn the luxuriant altarpieces, tapestries, and paintings of the time. They were depicted as frolicking infants and were indistinguishable from classically derived Cupid figures. Like flocks of little birds, they swarmed around corners, windowsills, and entranceways. In one famous pilgrim's church in northern Bavaria, more than two hundred little rosy rococo angels cover the interior. According to contemporary theological taste, "the altar and the whole interior space was crowded with throngs of angels." It is a truly Bavarian vision of heaven. Angels, whose mysterious, otherworldly powers had been described in the Bible, were now reduced to ornamental details in the complicated schemes of the rococo. Religious art had reached a dead end.

At the same time the coming of radical historical and social change cast its shadow before it. The eighteenth-century Enlightenment had done away with religious speculation and expression. The very existence of angels was called into question. Reason was the new altar of revolution, and on it angels had no place. Angels disappeared from art in the blink of an eye as the French Revolution of 1789 and what followed rendered them obsolete.

Angels resurface at the beginning of the nineteenth century in the paintings of the Nazarenes, a German and Austrian school of religious painters who patterned themselves after Raphael and his Italian precursors. Their interpretations of pure and archaic forms led to solemn-looking angels with just a hint of the softness of young girls. Putti were banished from church decor. A new pictorial conception of angels was coming into being. In England, Dante Gabriel Rossetti became the founding spirit of Pre-Raphaelism. In his romantic painting *Ecce Ancilla Domini*, he offers us a wingless angel clothed in white: a striking blend of sensuality and purity.

Angels also gained a foothold in popular culture. Beneficiaries of new printing methods spawned by the Industrial Revolution, the middle class began to purchase art reproductions. They hung pictures of guardian angels on the walls of their children's bedrooms. Angels were now seen as protectors who would guide small children and keep them from harm. Much like the evolution of folk tales into fairy tales, what was once a powerful source of meaning for the whole community now became the rightful property of children. Angels also congregated in graveyards; great marble figures with outstretched wings were among the favorite funerary monuments of the Victorian age.

In our own century angels have become spiritual motifs and symbols. Paul Klee's *Angel of Death* and *Angel of History* are spirits marked by the burdens of humanity. Marc Chagall discovered in his dreamlike world winged angels who serve as a bridge between the supra-sensible and the concrete. In *Angel with a Palette,* he even made himself an angel.

The world of angels today is an open one. Pictorial representations are not constrained by conventional motifs. Everyone can encounter his or her own angel, where and in whatever form they wish. We are all free to believe or not believe. Nonetheless, most of us continue to derive our ideas about what angels are from the artistic representations that the tradition of Western art has handed down to us.

JOSHUA REYNOLDS. *Heads of Angels.* 1787. Tate Gallery, London. (Granger Collection, NY)

MARC CHAGALL. *The Parting of the Red Sea.* 1966. Private Collection, New York.

ANGELS IN THE OLD TESTAMENT

he Hebrew word for angel is "mal'akh," meaning messenger, and is used in the Old Testament for human as well as divine emissaries. However, the angels we are considering are wholly spiritual beings residing in heaven. As Mortimer Adler remarks "they may come to earth to perform their missions, but they never remain for long." The notion of an angel fallen or stranded on earth is an intriguing one. It forms the basis of Tolstoy's beautiful story "What Men Live By" and is certainly the inspiration behind Nicholas Roeg's haunting movie *The Man Who Fell to Earth*.

When an angel visits earth he assumes a human form, which masks in part his true nature. But the artist who hopes to portray angels must project onto them the most exalted conceptions of human beauty. The angel's true disposition is to turn towards God. But for the human actor in the drama meeting an angel is supremely meaningful.

The Old Testament describes many such meetings. Each is an occasion for an encounter or confrontation between the human and the divine worlds. This is a truly significant moment and creates the tension that is at the center of the great works of art that address Old Testament themes. It also underlies the most often depicted appearance of an angel in the New Testament, the Annunciation.

In the story of creation from the Book of Genesis, God assigns his cherubim to watch over Eden after He has driven Adam and Eve out of the garden. Angels appear "as three men" in the house of Abraham to announce the birth of his son Isaac. Later, when Abraham is about to slay Isaac, the Angel of the Lord prevents him from accomplishing the sacrifice. The angel calls out to him, saying, "Lift not thine hand upon the lad, neither do anything unto him: for now I know thou fearest God..." (Gen. 23:12). Jacob wrestles with an angel at night until morning's light and will not let him go until he receives a blessing. Jacob asks his name, but the angel withdraws and does not answer him. Jacob also has a dream about angels: "And he dreamed, and behold a ladder set up on the earth, and the top of it reached to heaven: and behold the angels of God ascending and descending on it" (Gen. 28:12).

Rembrandt's earliest known painting dramatizes an incident in Numbers concerning the sage Balaam and his ass. Faced with invasion by the Israelites, the King of Moab sends to Balaam to have him curse them. Balaam at first refuses but then agrees to come. On his way to Moab the Angel of the Lord appears to him three times. Balaam does not see the angel, but the ass on which he is riding does. With the angel's third appearance the ass tries to turn around. Balaam raises his hand to strike him but is prevented by the angel, who reveals himself, saying: " Behold I come forth for an adversary, because thy way is contrary unto me; and the ass saw me, and turned aside before me these three times; unless she had turned aside from me, surely now I had even slain thee, and saved her alive."

The story of Tobit and his son Tobias is found in the Apocrypha to the Old Testament. It was a favored subject of religious painting throughout the Renaissance, treated by Perugino, Andrea della Verrocchio (or a follower), Savoldo, and Pollaiuolo, among others. Tobit is old and blind. He sends his young son, Tobias, to collect a debt for him. Outside his door Tobias finds "Raphael the angel standing before him," though he does not recognize him as an angel. Raphael tells Tobias that he will act as a guide for him on the journey. In the course of their travels, Tobias comes across a large fish. Raphael instructs him to kill it. Later, again at his companion's behest, Tobias burns the fish's entrails and is saved from evil spirits. At the end of the story he returns home. The angel tells Tobias to lay the gallbladder of the fish on his father's eyes. He does so and the old man's sight is immediately restored. At this point the angel makes himself known to them, as "one of the seven angels who stand with the Lord."

In *The Celestial Hierarchy,* Dionysius describes the various purposes for which angels come to earth: "... it was the angels who uplifted our illustrious ancestors toward the divine, and they did so by prescribing roles of conduct, by turning them from wandering and sin to the right way of truth, or by coming to announce and explain sacred orders, hidden visions, or transcendent mysteries, or divine prophecies." Dionysius's words apply to almost all appearances of angels in the Old Testament.

The Archangel Michael Leads Adam and Eve Out of Paradise from *Paradise Lost.* 1695.   Milton's expressed intent in offering his epic poem to the public was "to justify the ways of God to man." *Paradise Lost* is a work peopled with angels, both uncorrupted and fallen. To many readers, Satan is the real hero of the poem. According to William Blake: "The reason Milton wrote in fetters when he wrote of the Angels of God and at liberty when of Devils and Hell, is because he was a true poet and of the Devil's party without knowing it."

However, the archangels Michael and Raphael both play important roles in the poem. This engraving illustrates the conclusion of the work. Adam and Eve, now resigned to exile, are led out of the garden by Michael, who holds a fiery sword. Cherubim descend from heaven to guard the entrance to Eden. Milton describes their departure: "[Adam and Eve] looking back, all th'Eastern side beheld / Of Paradise... Wav'd over by that flaming brand, the Gate / With dreadful Faces throng'd and fiery Arms."

REMBRANDT VAN RIJN. *Balaam's Ass*. 1626. Musée Cognacq-Jay, Paris.   *Balaam's Ass* is one of Rembrandt's earliest known paintings. The work shows the influence of his teacher Pieter Lastman, who treated the same subject. In the painting the Angel of the Lord blocks Balaam's path. Balaam's ass sees what his rider does not and swerves aside, which angers Balaam. The tableau captures the angel in the act of staying Balaam's hand as he is about to strike the ass.

The angel dominates the canvas. With an imposing gesture he intervenes decisively, almost violently, in the course of human affairs. The monumental quality is reinforced by the grouping of rocks in the background. Everything about the composition suggests the encounter between spiritual and worldly values.

REMBRANDT VAN RIJN. *The Sacrifice of Isaac*. 1635. The Hermitage Museum, St. Petersburg. (Artothek, Peissenberg, Germany)   *The Sacrifice of Isaac* was painted a decade after *Balaam's Ass*. Its psychological awareness and technical mastery clearly point to the artist's growing maturity. The focal point of the canvas is Abraham's face, as he is caught surprised by the descent of grace. He has been spared from carrying out a sacrifice that would have brought the generation of the people Israel to an end. The angel holds Abraham's right hand, while the prophet's left hand covers his son's face, creating a chain that is a visual affirmation of God's covenant with Abraham.

GUSTAV DORÉ. *Jacob Wrestling with the Angel.* 1866. (Granger Collection, NY)   The incident illustrated here by Doré is one of the most powerful and mysterious events narrated in the Old Testament. The biblical text is unclear as to exactly whom Jacob wrestles. The Masoretic text of the Old Testament tells us, "And Jacob was left alone; and there wrestled a man with him until the breaking of the day" (Gen. 32: 24 ff.). Jacob will not let go of his opponent until he receives a blessing. "And [Jacob's opponent] said unto him, What is thy name? And he said: Jacob. And he said, Thy name shall be called no more Jacob, but Israel: for thou hast striven with God and with men, and hast prevailed." Jacob is transformed by this spiritual struggle; out of it the nation of Israel is born.

SCHOOL OF AVIGNON. *Jacob's Ladder*. Ca. 1400. Musée de Petit Palais, Avignon. On leaving his father's house, Jacob is granted a dream in which he sees "a ladder set up on the earth, and the top of it reached to heaven; and behold the angels of God ascending and descending on it" (Gen 28:12). Then God appears to Jacob and promises to him and his descendents the land all around as far as he can see. This is the first time that God appears to Jacob. The ladder about which he dreams is a clear sign of God's watchful Providence and the connectedness of earthly and heavenly things. In the Gospel of John, Jesus identifies himself with Jacob's ladder. He says to his disciple Nathaniel, "In all truth I tell you, you will see the heavens open and the angels of God ascending and descending on the Son of man" (John 1:51).

JUAN ANTONIO ESCALANTE. *An Angel Awakens the Prophet Elijah.* Ca. 1667. Gemäldegalerie, Berlin.   The Prophet Elijah is one of the most powerful characters in the Old Testament. Both his beginnings and his end are shrouded in mystery. He steps onto the stage to rebuke Ahab, King of Israel, who, influenced by his wife, Jezebel, has reinstituted the worship of the god Baal. After triumphing over 450 prophets of Baal, Elijah is forced to flee into the desert to escape the vengeance of Jezebel. There, hungry and exhausted, he falls asleep under a tree. An angel awakens him and bids him eat and drink of the food and water he lays out before him. Elijah does so, falls asleep again, and again is awakened by the angel, who says, "Arise and eat; because the journey is too great for thee" (1 Kings 19:7).

Escalante was one of the leading painters of the high baroque period in Spain. This work is part of a cycle of paintings of Old Testament scenes and depicts Elijah's second awakening. The painting of the angel's first appearance hangs in the Prado in Madrid.

WILLEM DROST. *The Vision of Daniel.* Ca. 1650. Gemäldegalerie, Berlin. Willem Drost was one of Rembrandt's ablest pupils. His entire treatment of this subject resembles a drawing by Rembrandt, which may have been Drost's point of departure. The prophet Daniel tells of a vision he had by the banks of the Ulai River near Susa. In it a goat with one horn tramples on a ram with two horns. The angel Gabriel descends to interpret the vision for Daniel as portending the final days. Daniel describes the terror the angel inspires in him. The painter's focus is unmistakable: the angel and Daniel are strongly lit, the landscape around them recedes into shadow. The ram to which Gabriel points can just be made out on the far shore. The youthful angel gently places his arm on the prophet, whose face expresses conflicting emotions of fear and reverence.

MASTER OF PRATOVECCHIO. *Three Archangels with the Young Tobias*. Ca. 1440. Gemälde-galerie, Berlin.   This painting is not a representation of the story of Tobias, for in that story only one angel, Raphael, makes an appearance. Rather, as the distinguished art historian Ernest Gom-brich points out, Tobias has become an emblem that identifies Raphael. In this work they stand next to each other. To the right is Gabriel holding a banner whose partially faded inscription refers to the Annunciation, the event with which he is most closely associated. To the left is Michael, who, as is customary, holds a sword. Raphael was celebrated as a healer — his name means God has healed — but also as the patron saint of children. It is for this reason that Tobias is pictured as a child. The dramatic difference in size between Tobias and the angels hearkens back to the medieval practice of representing angels as larger than life.

ANTONIO POLLAIUOLO. *Tobias and the Angel.* Ca. 1460. Galleria Sabauda, Turin.
(Art Resource, NY)   The story of Tobias and the Angel was evidently a very popular one in the
quattrocento. Versions of it abound. The story is unusual in that its real protagonist is Raphael.
Nowhere else in the Bible does an angel play such an active part. A well-known painting from
Verrocchio's workshop (now in the collection of the National Gallery, London) treats the subject in a similar fashion to this work of Pollaiuolo. In both Tobias grasps the fish in one hand and
Raphael's arm in the other. The dog, who is specifically mentioned in the Apocrypha account as
their traveling companion, trots contentedly beside them. Pollaiuolo's use of the newly mastered
art of perspective conveys both the length and arduousness of their journey.

GERARD HORNEBOUT. *Nativity* from the *Breviary of Bona Sforza*. Ca. 1517. British Library,
London.

ANGELS IN THE NEW TESTAMENT

he drama that the Old Testament narrates takes place on an earthly stage, for it is concerned with the laws and the history of a particular nation. The New Testament has a stereoscopic focus. It tells on the one hand the story of the Incarnation, but it also discourses on heavenly things. God comes to earth in the person of Christ, and the angels assume human form in their visits to earth. The artist then could paint them, but the enterprise of rendering incorporeal forms in art, of making the invisible visible, presented a definite philosophical problem. Dionysius addresses this question in *The Celestial Hierarchy*. He begins by pointing out that scripture uses symbols to render divine realities comprehensible and to conceal the truth from those unworthy of it. Scripture sometimes describes heavenly things in glowing terms, sometimes using incongruities. One should not take either of these approaches literally, he reminds his readers, lest on the one hand one imagines "that the heavens beyond really are filled with bands of lions and horses, that the divine praises are, in effect, great moos, that flocks of birds take wing there," or that one should think that "heavenly beings are golden or gleaming men, glamorous, wearing lustrous clothing." However, he concludes, used rightly, "everything can be a help to contemplation."

Angels appear to Christ and his followers many times in the New Testament. Gabriel announces the birth of John the Baptist, as well as bringing word to Mary of the coming birth of Jesus. An angel appears to Joseph in a dream and instructs him on the divine origin of Mary's son. Angels play an important part in the Nativity. They tell the good news to the shepherds who are nearby, bringing the message of "peace on earth, good will to men." And in Christ's darkest hour, on the Mount of Olives, an angel is sent down by God to comfort and strengthen him.

An angel frees the disciple Peter from the prison in which he is confined, and another angel comes to Paul in prison and comforts him. An angel appears to the Roman captain Cornelius, telling him to seek out Paul. In the Book of Revelation, John is commanded by God to "take the little book which is open in the hand of the angel which standeth upon the sea and upon the earth." John approaches the angel and says: "Give me the little book. And he said unto me, 'Take it, and eat it up; and it shall make thy belly bitter, but it shall be in thy mouth sweet as honey'" (Rev. 10: 8–10). An angel with a trumpet appears. Three angels who function as messengers call out in loud voices. John sees "four angels standing on the four corners of the earth, holding the four winds of the earth, that the wind should not blow on the earth, nor on the sea, nor on any tree" (Rev. 7:1). The whole of Revelation is a book of angels. These heralds perform great deeds; they struggle with evil and overcome it. They are the embodiments of God's righteous anger. Finally, an angel guides John to a high mountain, where he is granted a vision of the "holy city, new Jerusalem, coming down from God out of heaven prepared as a bride adorned for her husband" (Rev. 21.2).

(Opposiite) **CARLO CRIVELLI.** *Annunciation with Saint Emidius.* 1486. National Gallery, London. The *Annunciation with Saint Emidius* was painted as an altarpiece for an order of Franciscans in the town of Ascoli Piceno. In 1482 the town received a grant for limited self-rule from the pope. Details in the work make reference to this fact, in a kind of counterpoint to the dominant religious motif. St. Emidius, who kneels beside Gabriel, is the patron saint of Ascoli. He holds a model of the town in his watchful care. The minutely detailed and highly ornamented surfaces and the compressed verticality of the canvas testify to Crivelli's technical virtuosity.

The Gospel of St. Luke tells us that the angel Gabriel was sent by God to Mary. He greets her, saying, "Rejoice, you enjoy God's favour. The Lord is with you." Mary is disturbed by the angel's words, but the angel goes on to tell her that she will bear the Son of the Most High and that she should name him Jesus. Having understood Gabriel's message she responds, "You see before you the Lord's servant, let it happen to me as you have said."

Gabriel's visit to Mary is one of the central events of the Gospel story; the church teaches that the Annunciation is the moment of Christ's conception. In the Old Testament, Gabriel predicts the coming of the Messiah to Daniel. So it is appropriate that Gabriel should announce His arrival to Mary.

The Annunciation was a favorite subject for artists throughout the Middle Ages, Renaissance, and baroque period and inspired some of the most beautiful paintings in the canon of Western art. The relationship between Gabriel and Mary is imagined in varying ways. Often the angel kneels to show subordination to the Mother of God. The Holy Spirit appears in the form of a dove or a shaft of light. Other common iconographic elements include lilies, which are symbols of Mary's purity, and the book that Mary reads, which represents the verse in Isaiah that was considered to prefigure the birth of Christ: "Behold, the young woman shall conceive and bear a son, and shall call his name Immanuel" (Isaiah 7:14).

(left) ARTIST UNKNOWN (Austrian). *Nativity.* Ca. 1486. Gemäldegalerie, Berlin.

(below) CHARLES LE BRUN. *Adoration of the Shepherds.* Ca. 1690. Louvre, Paris.

In the Old Testament, visitations of angels betoken a radical intervention in the lives of those who encounter them. The birth of Christ signals a new chapter in the participation by angels in human affairs. They come to earth to celebrate his birth, glorify the major events of his ministry, and comfort Him in his time of suffering. The different versions of the Nativity included here show the diversity with which this principal moment in the Christian story can be handled.

The touching devotional work by an unknown Austrian painter emphasizes the intimacy of God's descent into Incarnation. The painter shows only the upper bodies of the angels, following a conventional manner of denoting their incorporeity. The seraphim's wings are red, the cherubim's blue.

Charles Le Brun's *Adoration of the Shepherds* depicts the event in much grander terms. The host of angelic figures surrounding Mary and her child is portrayed as a heavenly audience present at the birth of a king. They play instruments and sing hymns of praise in keeping with the general air of rejoicing.

SANDRO BOTTICELLI. *Mystic Nativity*. 1500. National Gallery, London.   In 1498 the fiery preacher Savonarola was publicly executed in Florence. Botticelli was deeply affected by this event, and his unusual Nativity may have been painted in response to it. The artist combines in the same tableau three scenes: the Birth of Christ, the Adoration of the Shepherds, and the Visit of the Magi. In addition he presents us with a host of angels. Botticelli often intended that his works be read symbolically. At the bottom of the composition three solemn angels embrace three men while three devils scurry for cover. It has been suggested that the three men represent Savonarola and his two companions who were executed with him. The angels in their circular dance at the top of the canvas convey that sense of grace and harmony that is characteristic of this master's work.

FRA ANGELICO: *The Coronation of the Virgin.* Ca. 1430. Louvre, Paris.   Fra Angelico lived most of his long and productive life in Tuscany. He painted this large wooden altarpiece for the cloister of San Domenico in Fiesole. In the center of the work Mary, dressed in costly attire, kneels under a late Gothic baldachin, or canopy, surrounded by angels in long, flowing robes. The angels play musical instruments; two of them shout for joy. Fra Angelico paid careful attention to the clothing of his figures, and his heavenly celebration becomes a feast for the eyes.

(above) STEFAN LOCHNER. *Mary in a Rose Garden.* Ca. 1440. Rhenisches Bildarchiv. Wallraf-Richartz Museum, Cologne.   Albrecht Dürer was familiar with Stefan Lochner's great *Adoration of the Kings,* describing it as an "exceptional work painted by Master Stefan of Köln." The small prayer panel, pictured above, is an excellent example of Lochner's style. Mary sits on the ground to signify humility, her unicorn pin is a symbol of virginity. She sits in the midst of angels. Two hold up a golden brocade curtain behind her; seven childlike angels gather before her in adoration, four angels play stringed instruments and one a hand organ. The delicate coloration and natural posing of the figures create a lovely sense of intimacy.

(overleaf) ANDREA DELLA VERROCCHIO. *Baptism of Christ* (and detail). 1472–1475. Uffizi Gallery, Florence.   Andrea della Verrocchio was a renowned sculptor and goldsmith active in Florence in the last part of the fifteenth century. He is best remembered for his star pupil, Leonardo da Vinci. Verrocchio's *Baptism of Christ* was commissioned by the monks of Vallambrosa. Tradition has it that the master had Leonardo paint one of the two angels at the far left of the canvas, and possibly the background behind them. If this is true, it is the first known example of Leonardo's work. Vasari writes: "It was obvious that this was the best part of the picture, and Andrea resolved never to paint again because he had been outdone by one so young."

(left) GIOVANNI BATTISTELLO. *The Agony of Christ.* Ca. 1615. Kunsthistorische Museum, Vienna.

(below) IL GUERCINO. *Angels Weeping over the Dead Christ.* Ca. 1618. National Gallery, London. (Granger Collection, NY)

Battistello's painting depicts Christ in the garden of Gethsemane being comforted by an angel. Christ's entire posture eloquently expresses his resignation at the fate that awaits Him. The two figures emerge from an extremely dark background, in keeping with the somber nature of the moment.

Guercino offers us an impressive contrast in his handling of the two angelic mourners. One looks at Christ's recumbent body with a gaze of heavenly compassion; the other inconsolably hides his face in his hands. Fluid treatment of the human figure and intense emotionality are characteristics of the baroque style that both of these works exemplify.

RAPHAEL. *Christ on the Cross with the Virgin, St. Jerome, Mary Magdalene, and John the Baptist.* 1502. National Gallery, London. This early work by Raphael was painted for an altarpiece in the Church of San Domenico at Citta di Castello. Of all his works it is the closest to the style of his teacher Perugino. Vasari, who knew the altarpiece, says, "If [Raphael's] name was not written upon it, no one would believe it to be by Raphael, but rather by Pietro [Perugino]." Raphael's graceful angels are certainly reminiscent of those in Perugino's painting *The Virgin Adoring the Child* (also in the National Gallery, London), but those created by Raphael are more fully embodied than his master's.

Though angels are not specifically mentioned in the biblical accounts of the Crucifixion, they are traditionally represented as playing a part and are often shown holding the instruments of Christ's passion: the cross, nails, spear, or crown of thorns. Here they bear chalices that catch his blood, thus signifying the sacramental character of the painting.

ALONSO CANO. *Vision of St. John.* Ca. 1635. Wallace Collection, London.   Revelation begins with the statement that God "sent his angel to make it known to his servant, John." Angels are present throughout John's dazzling vision of the final days.

RAPHAEL. *Deliverance of St. Peter.* Ca. 1512. Vatican, Stanza d'Eliodoro. Raphael traveled to Rome to undertake the decoration of the Stanze (a series of state rooms) in the Vatican. He executed four works for the Stanza d'Eliodoro, each depicting a great victory for the church. Raphael relies on an innovative use of contrast between light and dark areas to elevate the episode of Peter's liberation from prison into a universal parable of redemption. This technical mastery allows him to dramatically illustrate the biblical account of Peter's deliverance, which reads: "Then suddenly an angel of the Lord stood there, and the cell was full of light" (Acts 12:7).

FRANÇOIS BOUCHER. *The Visit of Venus to Vulcan.* 1754. Wallace Collection, London.

SECULAR ANGELS

hroughout the Middle Ages, the Catholic Church was the dominant cultural force in European society. Popes exercised real political power, monastic orders promulgated the contemplative ideal, universities were church-run institutions. The Gothic cathedral is perhaps the most perfect summation of the mind and purposes of medieval life. In addition the church was the unrivaled patron of the arts. Under these circumstances it is hardly surprising that medieval art is first and foremost religious.

The Italian Renaissance marked a profound shift away from a society centered on religion. A number of reasons could be cited for this change. The political climate in Italy was determined by urban rather than feudal imperatives, giving rise to a more intellectually restless and cosmopolitan population. The development of classical scholarship created a new attitude toward the heritage of antiquity, one that found in the human-centered cosmos of Greece and Rome a counterweight to the otherworldly orientation of medieval Christianity. Scientific and geographic discoveries raised questions that shook old certainties. And schism, corruption, and spiritual exhaustion within the church itself provoked stirrings of dissent that would soon split Christendom.

The art of the time was an extremely sensitive barometer of all of these changes. With the invention in the middle of the fifteenth century of scientific perspective, painting discovered powerful new means to create lifelike pictorial compositions. The artist turned away from the contemplation of heavenly things and took the world around him as his model. The artist also found new patrons. The confraternities and the wealthy families were not as dogmatic as the church in their requirements; often artists worked under the guidance of humanist scholars who devised elaborately symbolic programs for their paintings.

This is not to say that Renaissance art is nonreligious in spirit or subject, nor that rampant secularism took hold overnight. On the contrary, the art of this period was deeply imbued with Christian doctrine and values, but there was a revolutionary change in attitude whose effects were just beginning to become evident. The Christian story was enacted in recognizable landscapes, and the actors descended from a spiritual plane to become fully embodied and of this world.

All of these trends are reflected in the portrayal of angels. The medieval image of an angel was a stern, monumental figure clothed in white. Early in the Renaissance a change in costume becomes evident. Angels are now seen dressed in rich, heavy garments, with jeweled clasps — regal dress by all means, but of the earth. Their relative size is reduced to a human scale. They are painted playing instruments or singing in choirs closely resembling the performance practices of the time. In short, they become humanized.

Beyond this, the Renaissance witnesses the beginning of a progressive unmooring of the figure of the angel from a strictly religious context. Devoid of its grounding in deeply held beliefs, the stature of the angel as a subject for art becomes diminished. The angel is now either used as allegorical emblem or is increasingly eroticized.

The eroticizing of the angelic figure is in part due to a coincidence in iconography (that is, in the way symbols are used in art). Winged figures from classical mythology began to intermingle with the Christian images of angels. Common characters in classical mythology — Hermes, Nike, and Thanatos, the God of Death — are all described as having wings. However, it was the Erotés, small naked cupids, that were adopted by artists for use in religious art. While these figures appear on early Christian sarcophagi, they disappear in the Middle Ages. Their return amounts to a reinventing of the angelic personality. These angels are imagined as playful, even mischievous. And while they convey a childish innocence — that quality of undivided adoration with which the child looks upon his mother — particularly when associated with the Virgin, they are a far cry from the awe-inspiring angels that are found in medieval cathedral sculpture and painting. They signal a step away from seriousness and solemnity.

A parallel development concerns the gender of angels. Whenever gender is alluded to in the Bible, angels are male. In the Old and New Testaments, angels are referred to with the male pronoun; there are no specifically mentioned female angels. Medieval depictions accord with this convention. In early medieval works angels are usually portrayed with beards. In the Renaissance, however, we encounter distinctly feminine angels. In Fra Angelico's painting of the Last Judgment (now in the Museo di Marco in Florence), a feminine angel embraces a monk in paradise. In Da Vinci's *Annunciation*, Gabriel has an unmistakably feminine cast. Indeed, Gabriel is often depicted as feminine, in keeping with the intensely personal nature of the Annunciation, which takes place in Mary's bedroom.

Angels become softer and more feminine on the one hand or virtually indistinguishable from little cupids on the other. The cherub, the little angel of love, replaces the cherubim, the guardians of Eden who brandish flaming swords. These developments coincide and are entirely consonant with a gradual merging of Christian and erotic imagery.

While the erotic allusions of such biblical texts as the Songs of Songs — a collection of love poems from the Old Testament — were not unknown in the Middle Ages, the sexual content was successfully sublimated. But in Renaissance and baroque art the concentration on the human body led in other directions. While the Renaissance humanist Lorenzo Valla talked about meeting in heaven an angel "who does not inflame but extinguishes lust," Bernini's *Ecstasy of St. Theresa* seems to have quite the opposite effect.

Seventeenth-century art can perhaps be best understood as an effort to balance religious and secular impulses, primarily through the use of allegory. The baroque era was marked, in the words of one art historian, by its "inveterate disposition to look for symbolic meanings in nature and art." The Counter-Reformation, along with the rise of science and rationalism, shattered the hegemony of the Church. The angel, as if trying to find a safe retreat from unfavorable winds, sought shelter under the aegis of allegory. Here angelic figures were used persuasively to embody psychological states, high ideals, and, eventually, political agendas. Perhaps as late as the mid-eighteenth century the angel still retained traces of its former glory, but deprived of a tradition that rendered it vital, it eventually became reduced to a stock allegorical emblem.

The religious revivals of the nineteenth century embodied in art by the Nazarenes in Germany and the Pre-Raphaelites and their followers in England hoped to recover an authenticity missing in industrial society, which they found in the medieval period. Simultaneously, a sentimental cult of angels took hold of the middle class. It centered mainly on children, whose status in Victorian England was being redefined, and also around remembrance of the dead: angels perch on funerary monuments with their outstretched wings enfolding the departed.

The Symbolist movement, which flowered at the end of the century, was deeply imbued with spiritual longing and nostalgia. Turning its back on the natural world and the pageant of modern life that inspired the Impressionists, it closeted itself with the products of its own imagination. The artist exploited a vocabulary of religious, mythological, and occult symbols coupled with an ambivalent sexuality. Symbolist angels seem to arise from the unconscious rather than descend from the heavens; they are no longer messengers but the message itself.

Twentieth-century art veered off in a different direction. The program of abstraction begun by Malevitch and Kandinsky reached for a spirituality in art that left no room for the angel. With the exception of Paul Klee and Marc Chagall, angels are absent from the body of work of the major modern artists. As we approach the millennium, the situation seems to be changing once again. Angels arrive in different guises: in movies and the theater their traces are hard to ignore. Calendars and posters display the powerfully conceived angelic portraits of earlier times. These intermediary figures seem to offer a hope of credible spirituality for those who feel far from God, and yet still need to find a meaning in the world in which they live.

(left) FRANCESCO ALBANI. *Adonis Led by Cupids to Venus* (detail). Ca. 1600. Louvre, Paris.

(opposite) ANTHONY VAN DYCK. *Virgin with Donors* (detail). Ca. 1627. Louvre, Paris.

Putti — small, unclothed, winged angels — are found on early Christian sarcophagi but are absent from the religious art of the Middle Ages. The Renaissance witnessed their return; they began to figure in both religious and mythological paintings. Raphael's use of putti in works such as the *Sistine Madonna* is evidence of their emerging popularity. Juxtaposing Albani's mythological painting with Van Dyck's religious one illustrates the overlapping of motifs. The rippling banner held aloft by Albani's cupids recalls the banners with religious inscriptions that angels often carry.

GIOVANNI BELLINI. *Virgin with Sts. Mark, Benedict, Nicholas, and Peter* (detail). Ca. 1500. Santa Maria Gloriosa die Frari, Venice. (Art Resource, NY) Bellini's gracefully posed little angels offer a musical tribute to the Virgin (not shown in this detail). The angels in this painting mark a transitional stage between earlier, more august forms and the putti figures. They are angelic children, but they are partially clothed and their wings are full and multicolored.

(above) HENDRICK VON BALEN. *The Judgment of Paris.* Ca. 1599. Gemäldegalerie, Berlin.

(opposite) SASSOFERRATO. *The Mystic Marriage of St. Catherine.* Ca. 1650. Wallace Collection, London.

These two paintings provide further evidence of the convergence of pagan and Christian iconography. In von Balen's treatment of the Judgment of Paris, the cupid figures await the imminent victory of their patroness, Aphrodite. Paris's choice will set in motion events that will lead to the Trojan War.

Sassoferrato's painting expresses a deeply felt religious devotion, but the putti at the upper right are virtually identical to cupids in any number of mythological tableaus. The story of St. Catherine's marriage to Christ is recounted in *The Golden Legend* by Jacob de Voraigne, a collection of stories about the lives of saints that was immensely popular in the Middle Ages and Renaissance.

(right) PETER PAUL RUBENS. *Madonna in a Garland of Flowers.* Ca. 1616. Alte Pinakothek, Munich. (Artothek, Peissenberg, Germany)

(overleaf) CARLO MARATTA. *Cupids with a Garland of Flowers.* 1670. Louvre, Paris.

In this painting and on the overleaf that follows, Rubens and Maratta provide us with a gallery of cherubs. Rubens paints them in a devotional context surrounding the Virgin; Maratta shows four little cupids frolicking against a lush floral background.

(above) LAURENT DE LA HYRE. *Astronomy*. Ca. 1650. Musée des Beaux-Arts, Orléans. La Hyre's allegorical portrait of Astronomy is a fairly straightforward example of symbolic representation. Every element in the painting — the books, the globe and instruments, even the colors the artist has chosen — reinforces the metaphor. The religious associations that the winged figure would have provoked a century earlier retreat into the background. *Astronomy* is based on reasoned observation; the angel has become an embodied idea devoid of any spiritual presence.

(opposite) RAPHAEL. *Study of an Angel for the Planet Jupiter in the Chigi Chapel.* Ca. 1513. Ashmoleon Museum, Oxford. Around 1513 Raphael received a commission to design a private chapel for Agostino Chigi, a wealthy Florentine. He planned the inside of the dome as a re-creation of the vault of heaven, using religious and mythological elements. At the apex of the dome is a roundel in which God and his angels look down from on high. Surrounding the roundel are eight compartments. Each contains one of the seven planets, represented by the appropriate classical divinity (the eighth compartment houses the fixed stars). Above each mythological figure is an angel who guides the planet in its course. Raphael's *Angel for the Planet Jupiter* urges the planet onward with a dynamic gesture.

One notes the ease with which Raphael blends religious and classical elements. The idea that intelligences govern the planets is an Aristotelian one, on the surface compatible with Christian teaching. But its deeper implications are quite the opposite. On the whole this work and many that followed it had the effect of blurring the specifically religious significance of angels.

ALBRECHT DÜRER. *Melancholia*. 1514. Kupferstichkabinett, Berlin.   The work takes its name from the banner held by the bat in the upper left-hand corner. It is without question one of Dürer's most powerful creations, masterful in its technique and fluent in its use of allegory. The Renaissance idea of melancholy was complex. It was associated with the planet Saturn in medicine and astrology and was seen as having a beneficent influence on artists, statesmen, and theologians. The abundant symbolism points to its double nature. Symbols such as the bat and the emaciated dog express its negative, wasting character, while the industrious cherub seated to the right of the presiding figure suggest its more positive side. Here again the angelic figure is allegorically linked to cosmic rather than spiritual forces.

GIOVANNI BAGLIONE. *Heavenly Love Conquering Earthly Love.* Ca. 1602. Gemäldegalerie, Berlin.
Baglione was well known as the author of biographies of artists. As a painter he was influenced
by Caravaggio. Here he has created an impressive work about the struggle between two forces.
The two winged figures are placed in stark contrast. One, Earthly Love, is unclothed and lies on
the ground in a posture of defeat, while the full height of the canvas is taken up by the victorious
angel of Heavenly Love, clad for battle. Earthly Love stretches out his right hand in submission.
Titian, in his celebrated painting *Sacred and Profane Love,* treats the same theme somewhat differ-
ently. (In his painting Sacred Love is nude while Profane Love is richly attired.) However, the
composition of this work most closely resembles portrayals of St. Michael and the dragon.
Baglione distances himself from the religious content associated with this motif by treating the
subject as allegory.

(above) PETER PAUL RUBENS. *The Apotheosis of Henri IV and the Proclamation of the Regency of Marie de Medicis on May 14, 1610.* Ca. 1622. Louvre, Paris.

(opposite) ELISABETH-LOUISE VIGÉE-LEBRUN. *Portrait of Prince Henry Lubomirski.* Ca. 1789. Gemäldegalerie, Berlin.

Rubens's work is part of a cycle of twenty-one paintings, now in the Louvre, that was designed to glorify Queen Marie de Medicis. Renaissance art had begun the process of bringing the divine down to earth; the baroque saw a corresponding elevation of the human into the divine in its glorification of the monarchy. The king and queen are presented as gods.

Throughout the cycle, putti serve as attendants for the royal couple, testifying to the divine right by which the monarchs ruled and their celestial grandeur. Rubens's artistic excellence disguises the fact that the paintings are in the final analysis masterpieces of flattery. He was followed by a host of other artists of lesser magnitude trying similarly to exalt their own patrons.

Vigée-Lebrun's portrait of a young prince, painted the first year of the French Revolution, takes this genre as far as it was destined to go. The momentous events of that year destroyed the credibility of a divinely sanctioned monarchy. This work can be read as a sort of visual pun in which the metaphoric becomes literal. The prince is acknowledged to possess an angelic beauty and so he becomes an angel. The androgynous quality of the portrait reflects the increasing sexual ambiguity associated with the angelic figure.

(overleaf) FRANÇOIS BOUCHER. *Autumn.* 1745. Wallace Collection, London.   This painting was engraved by Duflos under the title *Erigone Vaincue,* referring to an amorous conquest by Bacchus. Boucher's art was a perfect reflection of court life under Louis XV. His cherubs are rationalized emblems of pleasure and ease. Here Eros has become thoroughly conventionalized, reduced in fact to ornament.

(opposite) WILLIAM ADOLPHE BOUGUEREAU. *Cupidon.* Ca. 1875. (Bridgeman Art Library, London)

(left) PHILIP REINAGLE. *Cupid Inspiring the Plants with Love.* 1797. Fitzwilliam Museum, Cambridge.

(below) ALEXANDRE CABANEL. *The Birth of Venus.* 1863. Musée d'Orsay, Paris.

Boucher had brought the figure of the angel into a cul-de-sac. Curiously, it was partly through their association with erotic energies that angels would reinvigorate themselves. Bouguereau's androgynous youth seductively folds his wings, emphasizing rather than concealing his nakedness. This angel would have shocked even Bernini. Cabanel's *Birth of Venus* is a modern treatment of a conventional theme. Cupid figures, angels of love, surround Venus, who according to myth was born out of the sea foam. The angels sport around the newly emerged goddess, and in a sort of pagan version of the Nativity they annouce the glad tidings of love. Reinagle's painting picks up on this same theme; his treatment is, however, less conventional. Even the vegetal world responds to the power of Eros. Clearly both Reinagle's and Cabanel's paintings depict the awakening of sexual energies. These same angels would soon be whispering their endearments to Freud and ushering in a new era of sexual freedom.

WILLIAM MORRIS (from a design by Edward Burne-Jones). *Vision of the Holy Grail.* Ca. 1890.
Birmingham Museum, Birmingham. The mid-nineteenth century witnessed a Gothic revival that
was spearheaded in England by the Pre-Raphaelite painters. The Middle Ages were idealized as a
time of faith and heroic action, and the Arthurian legends were found to be a practically inex-
haustible source of literary and artistic themes. Burne-Jones in his design for this tapestry follows
a very precise symbolic program. The Grail is of course a symbol with multiple meanings. Visiting
the Grail chapel are three knights. Bors and Perceval, who have not reached the highest perfec-
tion, kneel on the outskirts of the chapel, with three angels interposed between them and the
inner sanctuary before which Galahad kneels. Only he has proven himself worthy of the fullest
attainment of the mystery. Three other angels stand behind the altar as guardians of the Grail.

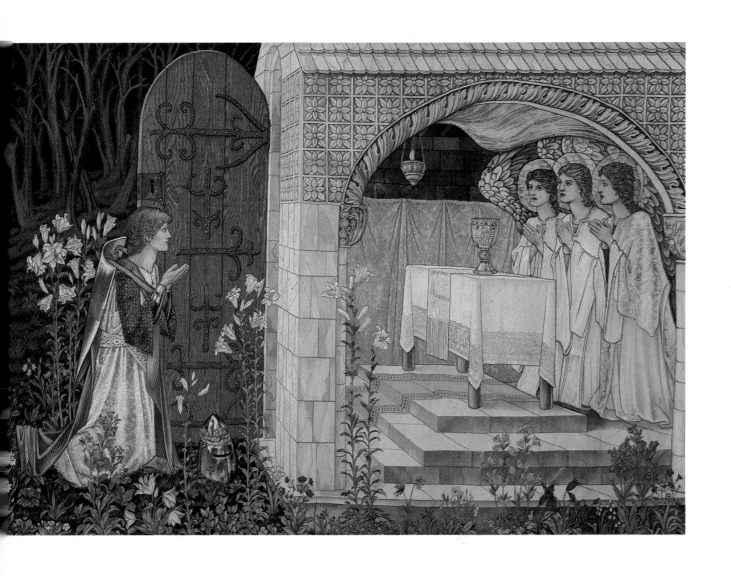

CARLOS SCHWAB

(opposite) CARLOS SCHWABE. *Spleen et Ideal* from *Les Fleurs du mal.* 1898. (Art Resource, NY)   Symbolist art arose late in the nineteenth century as a reaction against Impressionist and naturalistic styles of painting. Its practioners turned their backs on modern life and produced rarefied works that sought to recover mystical and mythological significances from the world of the unconscious. In so doing, the Symbolists created their own genre of angelic figures, such as the one pictured here: creations that express spiritual longings but at the same time are steeped in an uneasy eroticism. Schwabe's *Spleen et Ideal* is one of his illustrations for Baudelaire's *Les Fleurs du mal,* which was the seminal text for the Symbolist movement.

(right) ELIHU VEDDER. *The Cup of Death.* Ca. 1885. Fine Arts Museum, Richmond, Virginia. (Granger Collection, NY)   The Angel of Death is a common figure in rabbinical writings; Gustav Davidson's *Dictionary of Angels* mentions twelve angels by name who were said to serve this function. In the Gospel of Luke, Jesus tells the parable of Lazarus and the rich man. When Lazarus dies, angels carry his soul into Abraham's embrace. Christian tradition usually assigns to the archangel Michael the role of leading the souls of the dead into heaven. Classical Greek mythology personifies death as a winged figure named Thanatos. Vedder's portrait draws upon this rich vein of allusions as well as showing clear parallels to the emerging style of elaborately designed funereal monuments, which prominently featured large-scale angels.

(above) IGNAZ GUENTHER. *Guardian Angel*. 19th century. Burgersaal, Munich. (Foto Marburg, Art Resource, NY)

(opposite) J. H. S. MANN. *Guardian Angels*. Ca. 1860. Haynes Fine Art at the Bindery Galleries. (Bridgeman Art Library, London)

The devotion to the guardian angel became widespread during the Counter-Reformation. Its comforting presence was a powerful weapon in the church's armory against the forces of Protestantism. In the seventeenth century Pope Clement X gave this figure the seal of doctrinal approval. According to church teachings, every soul is assigned an angel at birth to watch over and guide it.

Guardian angels are usually associated with children. The biblical prototype is found in the story of Raphael and Tobias, which we have already discussed. But gradually, artistic representations detached themselves from any specific iconographic context. The angel was simply shown watching over the child or holding its hand. With the advent of mass art reproductions in the nineteenth century, angels found their way into the homes of the middle class. A quotation from the popular nineteenth-century guide *Sacred and Legendary Art* shows how attached the Victorians were to the idea of the guardian angel: "It would require the tongues of angels themselves to recite all that we owe to these benign and vigilant guardians. They watch by the cradle of the new-born babe, and spread their celestial wings round the tottering steps of infancy... Wonderful the fervour of their love who endure from day to day the spectacle of the unveiled human heart with all its miserable weaknesses and vanities..."

The guardian angel was particularly favored by mothers afraid for the health and well-being of their children. Pictures of angels were hung over children's beds. Along with the other gods and heroes of mythology, the majestic figure of the angel was now relegated to the nursery.

JOHN MELUISH STRUDWICK. *An Angel.* Ca. 1900. Roy Miles Gallery, London. (Bridgeman Art
Library, London)   This turn-of-the-century angel shows a distinct Pre-Raphaelite influence. The
painted niche in which it stands clearly alludes to the medieval sculptural tradition. Pretty angels
of this sort were very popular during the Victorian era.

PAUL KLEE. *Angel Still Feminine*. 1939. Paul Klee Foundation, Bern.   Klee's angels are extraordinary creations. With the exception of Chagall, he was the only major twentieth-century artist to probe their meaningfulness as symbols for contemporary life. In 1939, the year war was declared in Europe and only two years before the artist's death, Klee created an outpouring of angelic portraits. His angels are neither spirit nor human. Rather, they stand on a threshold. *The Angel Still Feminine* has yet to shed her humanity. As with all of Klee's angels, she remains in the process of becoming.

MASTER OF THE LIFE OF THE VIRGIN. *Coronation of the Virgin.* Ca. 1465. Alte Pinakothek, Munich. (Art Resource, NY)

ANGELIC MUSICIANS

T he late-medieval humanist Johannes Tinctoris noted that when painters wished to show their joy in heavenly things they painted angelic musicians. This motif became popular early in the Renaissance. Angels are shown singing in choirs and playing on contemporary instruments. These are depictions of angels in their heavenly state. Their music is played for the glory of God. As the Psalm says, "They praise in chords, and with organ" (Ps. 150:4). Their music is also dedicated to the Virgin Mary; depictions of the Coronation of the Virgin, such as Fra Angelico's, include hosts of angelic musicians.

Portrayals of angelic musicians indicate the delight and importance that music held for Renaissance society. Representations of angelic musicians began to faithfully reflect the actual performance practice of the time. These pictures are an invaluable source of information about the way musicians and singers arranged themselves in concerts, shedding light on solo, choral, and instrumental music. Early representations, for example, do not show angels reading music. This is first seen in the fifteenth century, but it is almost always associated with vocal music. In a painting by Bellini dating from the beginning of the sixteenth century small angels playing on instruments read from sheet music, corresponding to the emerging importance of instrumental music.

During the Renaissance the Netherlands was renowned for its music, and Netherlandish art produced some of the most memorable depictions of angelic musicians. Ghent, where Van Eyck painted his magnificent altarpiece, *The Adoration of the Lamb,* was one of the major centers of musical performance and composition. In this work Van Eyck shows in loving detail his own experience of music as it existed in his time, while offering a picture of the timeless quality of the heavenly songs of glory. Realism and symbolism here are joined together.

Angelic musicians held forth the promise that heaven would in some respects correspond to the world people lived in. Painters such as Bosch and Van Eyck picture heaven as a garden in which couples stroll beside fountains, sometimes serenaded by angels. The Christian could look forward to Paradise that preserved in a more perfect way the most beautiful aspects of human life; there he or she would be transported for eternity by heavenly music.

ROSSO FIORENTINO. *Angel Musician.* Ca. 1520. Uffizi Gallery, Florence. (Bridgeman Art Library, London)

SIMON MARMION. *Choir of Angels* (detail). Ca. 1459. National Gallery, London. Simon Marmion's *Choir of Angels* covers one panel of a large altarpiece painted for the Abbey Church of St. Bertin in St. Omer, France. The panel directly underneath it shows a church in which an episode from the life of the saint is set.

(opposite) CARLO SARACENI. *St. Cecilia with an Angel.* Ca. 1660. Galleria Nazionale di Arte Antica, Rome. (Granger Collection, NY)   St. Cecilia was believed to have lived in the second or third century. Her strict adherence to a vow of chastity and the miraculous happenings surrounding her martyrdom made her a powerful example of Christian piety and sanctity throughout the Middle Ages. During the Renaissance she became recognized as the patron saint of music. In Saraceni's painting she is about to play on the lute to the accompaniment of an angel who holds a double bass. Other instruments are scattered around them and a book of sheet music is open at their feet. The work shows how, in the latter part of the Renaissance, paintings of angelic musicians reflected current musical performance practice. Here St. Cecilia and the angel seem to be conferring before launching into their concert.

(below) FRA ANGELICO. *Coronation of the Virgin* (detail). Ca. 1430. Louvre, Paris.   This detail from Fra Angelico's *Coronation of the Virgin* shows part of a great celestial pageant. Saints, who have been given identifying attributes, and angels playing various instruments surround the central figure of the Virgin, who kneels to accept her crown. The angels here are not pictured as messengers or intermediaries, but are shown as eternal celebrants of the glory of God.

(above) HANS MEMLING. *Musician Angels.* Ca. 1485. Koninklijk Museum, Antwerp.   Following Van Eyck and his contemporary Roger van der Weyden, Hans Memling was the leading proponent of the school of Northern painting. This work is part of a triptych in which angelic singers and musicians surround the crowned figure of Christ as the eternal source of grace. The angels play in concert on a variety of accurately depicted contemporary instruments.

(opposite) JAN VAN EYCK. *Adoration of the Lamb* (detail). 1432. St. Bavo, Ghent. (Granger Collection, NY)   The angelic musicians pictured here constitute one panel of an altarpiece known as the *Adoration of the Lamb.* When opened, the altarpiece consists of twelve panels that, taken as a whole, present a late-medieval vision of paradise. The design is highly symmetrical; the angelic musicians to the right of the central panel are balanced by an angelic choir to its left. The musicians accompany the choir; the organist plays while the other musicians wait their turn. Their inclusion in the altarpiece reflects Ghent's importance as a center of musical composition and performance. The technical virtuosity, powerful iconography, and intensely realized mystical naturalism make Van Eyck's painting one of the crowning masterworks of Western art.

ASSOCIATE OF DA VINCI. *Angel in Red with Lute.* Ca. 1490. National Gallery, London.

ASSOCIATE OF DA VINCI. *Angel in Green with Vielle.* Ca. 1506. National Gallery, London.

In 1483 Leonardo da Vinci received a commission to paint an altarpiece that was to be installed in a new chapel built for the Milanese Confraternity of the Immaculate Conception. Leonardo had just arrived in Milan at the invitation of Duke Ludovico; this was his first major commission in that city. Leonardo began work on what was to become the *Madonna of the Rocks* with the expectation of completing it the following year. However, things did not go as originally planned.

The completion date of the first version of the painting, which now hangs in the Louvre and is reproduced in the introduction to this book, was well into the 1490s. In 1499 there was a dispute over payment, and Leonardo and his assistant refused to turn the work over to the confraternity. A settlement finally was reached in 1503. Leonardo agreed to furnish a copy as well as the original. The copy was used for the altarpiece and is now in the National Gallery in London.

The two musician angels were painted for the side panels of this altarpiece. The vicissitudes in accomplishing the commission explain the fact that these two angels, while clearly companion pieces, were painted sixteen years apart. Though their graceful postures and flowing robes are in harmony with the central panel, flaws in their execution strongly suggest that they were painted by one of Leonardo's assistants from his design.

GIOVANNI BELLINI. *The Doge Barbarigo, St. John, and Musician Angels (detail).* Ca. 1500. S. Pietro di Murano, Venice. (Scala/Art Resource, NY)   Giovanni Bellini was acknowledged to be the finest painter working in Venice in the second half of the fifteenth century. Dürer met the aged Bellini and shared this high opinion of the painter. Bellini was the brother-in-law of the pioneering artist Mantegna, who influenced his early work. But Bellini's more mature style captures a sense of inwardness lacking in the work of his predecessors.

In fifteenth-century Venice, art served purposes that were not solely religious. It also had the political function of glorifying the city and its leaders. Here the angelic violinist is ostensibly on hand to join the Doge in honoring St. John. In fact the central position of the Doge in the canvas gives him a place of honor.

MATTHIAS GRÜNEWALD. *The Isenheimer Altarpiece* (detail). 1510–1515. Musée d'Unterlinden, Colmar.   The *Isenheimer Altarpiece* was commissioned by the Antonite commandery of the Cloister of Isenheim. It is one of the most elaborate works of its kind. When it is closed it depicts the Crucifixion flanked by side panels of St. Anthony and St. Sebastian. Opened the central panel is divided into two parts. To the right is a light-filled Nativity, to the left a joyous concert of angels painted against a dark background. Side panels present the Annunciation and the Last Judgment. The altarpiece can be opened a second time, revealing the sculpted figures of St. Athanasius and St. Jerome in between painted panels of the temptation of St. Anthony and a meeting of St. Anthony and St. Paul.

   Grünewald's angelic musicians are highly idiosyncratic. They are situated in a chapel where they serenade the Virgin Mary, who, wearing a crown, kneels between two columns slightly to their right. In the middle ground an angel clothed in red, the color of love and virginity, plays a viola. Beside him a mysterious angel covered in feathers with green wings, to signify hope, plays a bass lute. In the foreground an angel clothed in white plays the viola da gamba. This last angel cannot by any stretch of the imagination be considered beautiful, yet his countenance is radiant with joy. Behind the three main performers a flock of childlike angels each with his own distinct personality, gaze upon the scene in rapture.

PIERO DELLA FRANCESCA. *St. Michael.* Ca. 1469. National Gallery, London. (Granger Collection, NY)

MICHAEL AND THE LAST JUDGMENT

The archangel Michael, known as St. Michael by the Catholic Church, is the most venerated of all the angels. In fact he was the first angel to whom the church granted a special liturgical observance.

According to the Christian tradition, the history of the world is bounded by two great events: the War in Heaven and the Last Judgment. The War in Heaven ends with Satan and the rebel angels being cast down to Hell and sets the stage for man's fall and redemption. The Last Judgment brings all history to a close. In both of these pivotal episodes Michael plays a leading role.

Michael's battle with Satan is described in Revelation: "And now war broke out in heaven, when Michael with his angels attacked the dragon. The dragon fought back with his angels, but they were defeated and driven out of heaven. The great dragon, the primeval serpent, known as the devil or Satan, who had led all the world astray, was hurled down to the earth and his angels were hurled down with him" (Rev. 12:7–9).

This passage has furnished the inspiration for numerous paintings and sculptures. *The Princeton Index of Christian Art* makes mention of over 900 works prior to the year 1400 devoted to this theme, and it continued to fascinate artists throughout the Renaissance and baroque periods. These works celebrate Michael the warrior and served to support the church in its more militant aspect. Michael could be seen as leading a crusade or defending the church from heresy. Beyond specific historical applications, the dramatic quality inherent in this struggle between the forces of light and darkness provided artists with abundant inspiration.

The second role that Michael is commonly presented as playing is as the weigher of souls on the Day of Judgment. Although the Bible does not specifically mention him in this context, he was early on associated with the souls of the dead. An Apocryphal text, *The*

Testament of Abraham, relates that Michael is so powerful that his intercession can rescue souls from damnation. This idea was taken up in the Catholic Church. At one time the liturgy for the dead contained the prayer, "May Michael the standard bearer lead them into the holy light."

Michael was the subject of a widespread cult in the Middle Ages. Its roots lay in the Near East where he was called upon for aid in times of sickness. In the early Middle Ages in Italy, during a time troubled by invasion and uncertainty, Michael was reported to have appeared on Monte Gargano. This report gained wide currency and helped the growth of his cult in western Europe. In fact his cult became so popular that the church for a time declared it heretical, only to allow it to be revived later. Churches dedicated to Michael were popular goals of pilgrimage. The most famous of these is the mighty Gothic master-piece Mont St. Michel, on the coast of Normandy.

Michael's prominent position and identification with the struggle between light and darkness suggests a kinship with other mythological heroes. His first appearance in the Bible is in the Book of Daniel, where the prophet has a vision of the final days. An angel tells Daniel: "And at that time shall Michael stand up, the great prince who standeth for the children of thy people" (Dn. 12:1). Endowed with power and mystery, Michael is the anti-dote to trivial conceptions of angels as flocks of sweet, cloying cherubs. He is the perfect embodiment of the triumphant nature of truth.

HIERONYMOUS BOSCH. *St. John on Patmos.* Ca. 1485. Gemäldegalerie, Berlin.   Hieronymous Bosch is best considered as a primitivist Renaissance painter. The twentieth-century surrealists saw him as a modern, kindred spirit, but in fact he looked back to the Gothic period for his primary source of inspiration. The visionary quality of the Book of Revelation strongly appealed to him. His St. John is pictured at the moment of receiving his vision from the angel; he is about to put pen to paper. The blue angel is an unmistakably Boschian creation, with its strange insectlike wings. Blue is the color of the cherubim, whose purpose is to know God and, in Dionysius's words, share that knowledge "with an outpouring of wisdom."

(left) LUCA GIORDANO. *The Archangel Michael Flinging the Rebel Angels into the Abyss.* Ca. 1655. Kunsthistorisches Museum, Vienna.

(opposite) RAPHAEL. *St. Michael Trampling the Dragon.* Ca. 1518. Louvre, Paris.

St. Michael's victory over Satan is the subject of numerous works whose diverse treatments reflect changing artistic aims, but the dynamic contrast between the forces of good and evil animates all depictions of this spiritual conflict.

Raphael painted this large St. Michael toward the end of his life. The archangel is a figure of classical beauty. His costume and aspect deliberately recall ancient Roman models. The figure of Michael epitomizes for the artist the parallels between the grandeur of Rome and the church triumphant. Every aspect of the work builds on the contrast between the two figures. Michael is dazzlingly lit; the devil grovels in darkness. The splendidly realized graceful turn of the angel stands in marked contrast to the twisted shape of his opponent. Michael's delicate, multicolored, feathery wings catch the movement of the air. Satan's leathery ones hang on his back like weights to drag him farther down.

Giordano's high-baroque work uses other means to paint the opposition between spiritual and irrational forces, emphasizing the emotional contrast between Michael's serene, aristocratic visage and the horror-struck faces of the fallen angels. The fiery red at the bottom of the canvas is graduated into a warm, suffused glow at the top. It is of note, however, that the demons occupy more of the canvas here than in Raphael's work. For the baroque period the powerful forces of the unconscious, once cast into outer darkness, were more insistent and less easily put down.

(above) PAPYRUS OF ANI. *The Weighing of the Heart.* Ca. 1350 B.C., from *The Egyptian Book of the Dead.* ©1994 James Wasserman, Chronicle Books, San Francisco.

(opposite) KARTNER MEISTER. *St. Michael Weighing Souls.* Ca. 1480. Gemäldegalerie, Berlin.

Michael is given two sacred functions: battling the Devil and weighing the souls of the dead on the Day of Judgment. The weighing of souls is an ancient motif, clearly present in Egyptian art, where the souls of the dead or the initiate are weighed in the balance against a feather, symbol of the goddess of truth and righteousness, to see if they are worthy.

In Western paintings, such as this monumental study by an anonymous fifteenth-century German master, Michael holds the scales in his left hand. On one side of the balance is the naked human soul, on the other its heavy accumulation of sin, which is being dragged down by a demon. The Kartner Meister's treatment deals with both of Michael's roles. As he assays the worth of the human petitioner, he is poised to slay the demon that seeks to bring the soul into damnation.

(above) ALBRECHT DÜRER. *Angel with the Key to the Bottomless Pit.* 1498. Kupferstichkabinett, Berlin.

(opposite) ALBRECHT DÜRER. *St. Michael Fighting the Dragon.* 1498. British Museum, London.

In 1498 Dürer published a series of woodblock prints illustrating the Book of Revelation with the text running on the verso of each print. The late-fifteenth century was a time of apocalyptic fears and expectations. In this same year, the Italian monk Savonarola, who preached that the end of the world was nigh, was exectued at the stake in Florence.

Dürer's deeply disturbing work has had a lasting influence on German art and culture. It depicts St. John's revelation in meticulous detail. Dürer's unequalled command of line indelibly impresses these fantastic visions on the viewer's imagination.

St. Michael Fighting the Dragon is distinguished by Dürer's vigorous handling of a motif that, as we have seen, is a common one in medieval and Renaissance art. The peaceful valley at the bottom of the picture forcefully contrasts with the bloody battle raging above.

In *The Angel with the Key to the Bottomless Pit,* the angel is locking a very tame-looking dragon into the abyss. Meanwhile, an angel vouchsafes St. John a vision of the New Jerusalem, which looks much like a late-medieval Flemish town. This print, which closes the series, conveys a sense of calm resolution after the furious barrage of imagery that precedes it.

(above) The Second Trump. Illumination from the Apocalypse of St. Severin. 13th century.

(opposite left) PETRUS CHRISTUS. *The Last Judgment* (detail). Ca. 1452. Gemäldegalerie, Berlin.

(opposite right) HANS MEMLING. *The Archangel Michael.* Ca. 1480. Wallace Collection, London.

Memling's painting of St. Michael holding his sword is in serene counterpoint to those works that emphasize his more militant aspect. Memling's works do not vibrate with the same religious fervor as those of some of his contemporaries. Indeed, one critic has described a niche painting of his showing Michael trampling on the dragon as more of a dance than a battle. Here the archangel's untroubled gaze looks out at the viewer with penetrating intelligence. Memling brings to bear the naturalistic and highly refined style he employed to paint human subjects to create a kind of angelic portraiture.

MICHELANGELO. *The Last Judgment*. 1536–1541. Sistine Chapel, The Vatican. (Granger Collection, NY)   Michelangelo's vision of the Last Judgment takes up one entire wall of the Sistine Chapel. Nearly thirty years before he had painted the story of Creation on the chapel's ceiling. Now, working in the same room, he addressed himself to the story of the end of all things. His *Last Judgment* is a dark and troubling work, reflecting his apprehension that man with his ineradicable flaws has only one hope, the mercy of the Redeemer.

Michelangelo's first biographer, Ascanio Condivi, whose *Life of Michelangelo* was published during the artist's lifetime, was deeply impressed by *The Last Judgment*. He describes the angels that are reproduced here:

"In this work Michelangelo succeeds in expressing everything that painting can capture of the human body without neglecting any attitude or movement... [In the] central zone near the bottom there are seven angels described by St. John in the Apocalypse, who are blowing their trumpets from the four corners of the world. They call the dead to the Last Judgment. Two are holding an open book so that everyone can read and review the history of their lives and judge themselves. At the sound of the trumpets the tombs open and the bodies emerge with marvelous and diverse attitudes."

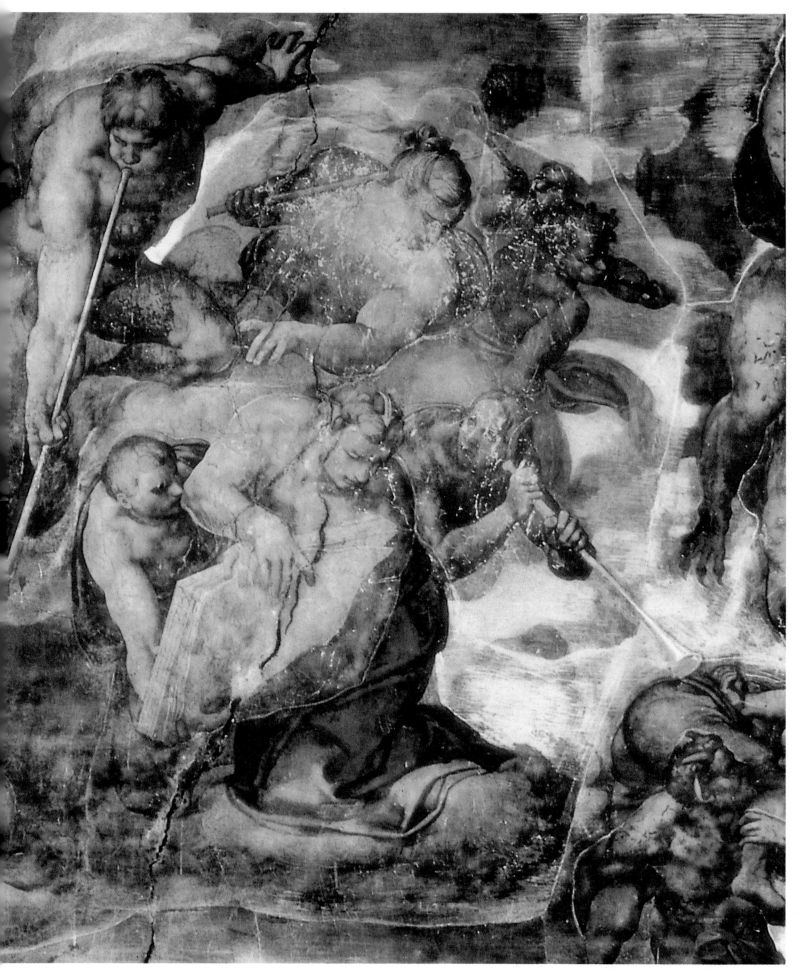